Floating Between Hospice and Heaven
Who Was He Talking To?
A True Story

Kate Benson

Copyright © 2020 Kate Benson

All rights reserved

ISBN No. 978-0-578-92787-9

"Did you talk to God last night?"
"Yes."
"What did He say?"
"Go to hell."

Introduction

When it comes to the subject of death and dying, stories of near-death experiences are plentiful. One story describes people seeing angels. That story details people hearing beautiful music just before death, and the next tells of people seeing relatives and loved ones who have long since passed over. Skeptics say these experiences are not proof of the existence of God, angels, heaven or life after death and are debunked through the science of the dying brain.

Floating Between Hospice and Heaven is not a story of a near-death experience. It is the story of a journey to 'death' and what happened along the way. Science cannot explain with certainty just who Bert Binghamton was talking to when he whispered, listened, nodded and whispered back as if in conversation.

My father's passing was not just another entry in the book of births and deaths. It was a spiritual wonder. Never, before or since, have I witnessed a more deeply religious and moving event. It was a long, three-day conversation my father had with God, heaven and the angels.

This telling is a true account of what took place, written by someone who was there. It is the story of a funny, kind, honest, gentle, faithful sinner and his brave and passionate quest to be with the Lord. Those with long and staunchly-held beliefs may find troubling some of the facts in this true story. Some with more loosely-held or borderline beliefs may find the facts enlightening and inspiring.

Everyone wants to know what happens when we 'die'. Everyone longs for proof there is something beyond, something more than birth-life-death and it's over. A breathtaking heaven and the fires of hell exist. I saw proof.

***

At the time of his death Bert still had all of his immediate family. This included his wife Jane and three grown children: Michael was the eldest, Dirk next, and daughter Kimberly was the youngest.

Michael and Dirk were each married. Michael was an engineer married to a priest, Helen. They lived in Syracuse, New York with their three children.

Dirk was a marketing expert married to a veterinarian, Lynn. They lived in Lexington, Kentucky with their one son, Jason.

Kimberly was not married and resided in Houston, Texas.

(Names and locations have been changed to preserve family privacy.) ***

Table of Contents

Chapter 1
The Man

Chapter 2
The Father

Chapter 3
The Denomination

Chapter 4
A Third Choice

Chapter 5
Saturday, March 21, Late Evening
A Realization

Chapter 6
The Beginning

Chapter 7
She Would Lift Me Up

Chapter 8
Go To Hell

Chapter 9
Last Call

Chapter 10
I Really Have To Go

Chapter 11
The After-ness

Chapter 12
A Fish and Unexpected Visits

Chapter 1

The Man

Bert Binghamton loved God, his family and his country. He was a little dude, just 5'10", and stocky. He was hairy too, with hair on his back and even his knuckles, but none on his head. He had gone bald in his twenties. He was a down-to-earth, practical, get 'er done kind of guy, athletic and fit. He had happy, hazel eyes and always smelled of tobacco smoke with a hint of Old Spice.

Bert was raised by a kind, gentle, unconditional woman with a rich belief in God. His father was withdrawn. Bert's IQ tested at 143. He skipped grades, entered college when he was 16, and graduated in three years. He served two tours in Korea in what was then the Army Air Corps.

After having three children with his wife Jane, Bert enlisted his architect father-in-law to design and build a house in the suburbs of Chicago. He thought it would be a healthy, safe place to raise a family, and it was. He carved out a good, upper-middle class life for his family in suburbia, complete with country club membership and golf and swimming lessons.

The overarching sentiment one will hear when asking people to remember Bert is how funny he was. A joke told by another would get some laughter. The same joke told by Bert would have people rolling around hysterical. He simply had a knack for making people laugh. He was a jokester but not a prankster. He was not the life of the party; he was the life of every party. He loved to entertain, and he was the king of the backyard barbecue.

Bert was a sharp dresser. He was a well-respected stockbroker with one of the larger firms in downtown Chicago. He had an admirably strong work ethic. Like so many of his generation, each morning he boarded the train to the city for work, and every night he rode the train back to the suburbs, always home for dinner. He rarely missed work, and was rarely sick.

He was a man faithful to God. He was not particularly religious as in quoting scripture, but he attended church every Sunday and most Wednesday nights. Nightly he read his lessons with the Bible and Mary Baker Eddy in his little chair under the reading lamp in his bedroom. He always made God a part of his children's lives. Not just in time of trouble, but daily. He lived his life with love for others. He communicated God's love through good humor. He did not lie, cheat, steal or do drugs. He was mostly optimistic and happy, sometimes cynical, but generally gentle and kind.

Bert was an exceptionally good dancer. He taught all his children to dance well. Bert loved animals, especially dogs. He was a good man with a pure heart who loved golf. In his world it was God first, family second, golf third.

Bert Binghamton also smoked, drank, cursed, and took the Lord's name in vain. He drove drunk. He rarely wore a seat belt. He gambled on just about everything except horses and dogs. He lost his temper on occasion, and once got in a fistfight with his teenage son. He was at times impatient and judgmental. He was racist; he refused to attend the wedding of a niece because it was a mixed-race wedding, and he threatened to pull his daughter out of college unless she agreed to break up with her boyfriend who happened to be black.

Bert was opinionated. He spoke ill of blacks and Jews and commies and chinks and wetbacks. He was bigoted against just about every group and a believer in every racial stereotype. He was derogatory but not hateful or malicious. You never really got the impression he meant insult or racism in his heart.

His funny, lovable side must have outweighed the rest because he was a highly-regarded, respected and extremely popular member of his community.

Bert was a big drinker. He was what is termed a 'functioning alcoholic.' His drinking never interfered with his work. He rarely drank in the daytime, but he drank all evening. When he threw parties he was always ready to get someone another drink so that while fixing their drink in the bar out of sight of his guests, he could make himself a drink, chug it, and make another to take back out to the party. Thus he could disguise how much he was actually drinking. He was a lovable drunk and never turned violent when drinking, never stumbled and fell, never passed out.

Bert the man had mischief in him

When he and his wife Jane were in the process of naming their last-born, daughter Kimberly, they couldn't agree on a name. They decided to put all the names in a hat and choose one at random. Bert wrote down the names on a slip of paper and tossed them into one of his hats. He shook it up and had Jane choose one. The name on the paper was Kimberly.

Later that day Jane was idly going through the slips of paper in the hat and soon realized something; all the slips of paper had "Kimberly" written on them.

Bert was a gentle, lovable soul, a simple man who, for all of his life, always did the best he knew how.

Chapter 2

The Father

Bert Binghamton was a loving, loyal, faithful husband and provider and a supportive and giving father of three. He taught his children to be thankful to God for everything. He taught them to say grace before every meal and to say their prayers every night. He taught respect for others, and to be polite to their elders, other kids and law enforcement. He did not tolerate drama.

Of course all meals commenced with giving thanks to the Lord for our food. Not all family members gathered for all meals, but Bert insisted the family have dinner together every night. During those meals he would hold spelling and grammar contests between the kids. These resulted in all three children being quite good at spelling and grammar. A good education was important to him, and he eventually sent all three kids to college.

He raised a modest family: no one was permitted to parade around in their underwear. If not dressed, it could be pajamas. All bedroom doors were closed at night.

On Christmas morning some parents allow their children to rip at will into what's under the tree. Not Bert. He said he would not have his kids acting like "a bunch of shrieking savages from the woods." The family opened gifts one at a time with Bert as acting Santa.

He made it a point to expose his children to those less fortunate, driving them through seedy parts of town with rundown buildings and littered streets. It was his best shot at having his children enter the world as adults with their eyes open, to "see how the other half lives."

He taught his kids what most parents teach their kids. He taught them about integrity. If you get married you stay married, and stay faithful to the end. If you give your word you keep your word, no matter what. If you make a promise you keep that promise, unconditionally. To educate them about the importance of building credit, he never bought cars for them. Instead, he loaned them money to buy cars and made sure they paid back every penny.

Bert loved animals. He taught his children how to love and be kind to them. He instilled in them a reverence for all life. He always made sure they had a dog to love and care for, and he took such good care of them and they lived so long that the family only had two dogs during their upbringing.

Bert saw to it the kids were enrolled in scouting and went to camp every summer. He gave them experience with not only scouting, but just about every sport imaginable, indoor and outdoor. The only exception was hunting. Except for a BB gun the boys used for target practice, there were never guns in the house.

Bert was against hunting. "Life is precious and should be respected, never shot and killed for sport." He said the senseless killing of God's creatures was wrong; the only time it would be justified would be for hunting food. These were not everyone's lessons, but they were his lessons.

He taught his kids to dance, sing, camp and fish, including cleaning and cooking the fish. Each year he rented a cabin on a lake where he took his family on vacation. He taught them about boating and water skiing safety.

Bert's wife Jane engaged in corporal punishment of the children only to an extent – slapping, smacking and washing out young mouths with soap. The task of the heavy-duty punishment was assigned to Bert.

When one of the children broke a rule during the day while Bert was at work, Jane waited until Bert got home and ordered him take the guilty party into their room and deliver their punishment: a hand-to-hinder spanking.

Bert cooperated. He took his daughter into her room and closed the door. Jane stood outside to listen and ensure that the job got done. Bert whispered to his daughter, "Make a lot of noise," and slapped his own thigh while his daughter yelled in 'pain.' When it was over, Jane was satisfied the punishment had been carried out.

This did not happen every time, but on more than one occasion. Bert often didn't see the point of such harsh punishment, particularly since the breach had occurred some seven hours earlier.

The secret of those 'spankings' would be kept forever between father and daughter.

When Bert caught his rebellious second son smoking out behind the garage, Dirk was in big trouble. That night at the dinner table a discussion about smoking heated up the conversation. The two argued.

Bert said, "I forbid you to smoke. Smoking is bad for you."

Dirk said defiantly, "Well *you* smoke."

"I can quit any time I want."

"So let's see you then."

Bert angrily snatched the pack of Lucky Strikes from his left shirt pocket, squashed it and what cigarettes were left and threw it hard onto the table.

"There," he said, "I quit."

He never again smoked another cigarette. After thirty years of smoking, he quit cold turkey simply to be an example to his son.

In winter Bert of course taught his small children how to build snowmen and make snow angels. When they got older he pulled them on their sleds behind the car on the school playground. He allowed them to build an ice rink in the back yard so they could skate all winter, and took them tobogganing every couple of weeks. At Halloween he turned the two-car garage into a scary and fun haunted house for all the kids in the neighborhood. At Thanksgivings while driving up north to visit relatives, they played games such as listing all the people who had to work on holidays or singing Christmas carols together.

Bert was an involved parent. He gave his children wholesome, fun, responsible, loving, protective, kind, adventurous upbringing with plenty of laughs along the way.

Chapter 3

The Denomination

Bert raised his children in the Christian Science faith. This church has no rituals like other religions do, not even baptism.

Bert was not the radical, fanatical purist you read about in the headlines who would rather let their children die than get help for them. Rather, he taught that Christian Science is simply a good health philosophy. It is about developing the power of the mind over matter. It is about asking God for healing first and if it doesn't come, visiting a doctor. "God created the doctors and He guides their brains and hands in their work."

When his children were sick with the flu or a cold and needed medicine, he provided the medicine they needed. At the same time, he ministered to them. In Bert's faith, man is created in God's image, perfect in every way. That includes good health. If that good health falters, it is evil invading the body.

As a pre-teen, Kimberly took ill with an unusually virulent case of influenza. She was only 11 when she had fever, diarrhea, vomiting and a violent cough. The doctors had done what they could and sent her home, advising that recovery would very likely take a long time.

Later that night as her Dad was tucking her in for the night, Kimberly complained about how awful she was feeling.

Bert asked her, "You're not sick when you're asleep, are you?"

"No."

"That's because you're not thinking about being sick when you're asleep. Do you remember in the Bible where it says, "Be not afraid"?

"Yes..."

The bad guy wants you to be afraid. Don't even give the evil thing power by acknowledging it. Deny it. Deny that it exists in you and you will feel better. It's mind over matter."

"Okay," Kimberly whimpered weakly through her tears.

"Trust God," Bert said, "trust God and know -- know in your *heart* -- that Jesus and all His angels will be right here in this room with you, watching over you all through the night. Will you do that?"

"I'll try."

"That's my girl." As he kissed her on the forehead she slipped into a deep and restful sleep. Comfort.

Silently he turned out the light, left the room and pulled the door closed behind him.

Oddly, just the very next morning Kimberly was feeling much better, and within just a few days she had fully recovered. The doctors were baffled at her quick recovery from such a serious illness. They had thought it would take weeks. They chalked up that little miracle to her youth.

When Bert was 60 he had a small heart scare. He was taken by ambulance to the emergency room, treated and released. A follow-up visit was scheduled with Bert's local doctor.

The forty-something doctor stood and leaned back on his desk, positioning himself so he towered over his seated patient.

"Mr. Binghamton, you sustained some damage to your heart muscle. I am prescribing for you some medication you will need to take for the rest of your life. It will be imperative that you limit all your physical activities from now on."

"What about golf?" Bert asked. "Will I be able to play golf?"

"No, I'm sorry," the doctor replied, "you will not be playing golf again, ever. It's just too strenuous."

"Not even if I take a cart and don't walk?"

"Not even if you take a cart and don't walk," the doctor parroted. Though he tried to hide it, condescending amusement crept into his fake smile.

'You will never play golf again' was not something even a doctor should say to Bert.

On the ride home Bert talked with Kimberly about his visit with the doctor.

"He told me I'll never play golf again. Can you imagine that? Well, that doctor is wrong, and I'm going to prove it."

And he did. Inside of six weeks he was back on the golf course, swinging, smiling and thumbing his nose at "that supercilious doctor". He made such a quick recovery it garnered an article in the local small-town paper.

His teachings of healing and the example he set carried down.

While tobogganing in his forties, Michael broke his back. The doctors said he would probably never walk again and if by some miracle he did, he would certainly never play golf again.

Like his father before him, Michael proved the doctors wrong. Within four months he was playing golf again as if nothing had ever happened. The doctors were mystified. They said cervical injuries to the spine could not heal that fast. They chalked up this little miracle healing to the patient being married to a priest.

In her late forties, Jane had contracted blood poisoning from a cut on the top of her foot. Medicine in that decade was not what medicine is today. A tiny line had begun moving up her leg. The doctor told her that it could stop on its own, but if it didn't and it reached her groin and the lymph nodes, she would die.

She was sent home. Bert was out of town at the time. She went to bed but could not sleep. She got up every so often to check the line's progress up her leg.

Soon it had reached her mid-thigh. While not a particularly religious person, she began to pray and pray hard. She did not want to die.

Just a short while later, what she described as a "light" came on inside her head. It filled her entire being. With the light an overwhelming sense of peace washed over her. It wrapped itself around her like a warm blanket and comforting arms. And it was then that she knew. She knew she had received a healing. She no longer felt the need to get out of bed to check the line because she just somehow "knew" it was gone. She sank into a deep sleep. When she awoke in the morning she found affirmation: the line had disappeared. She would be fine.

Over the years the Binghamton family members were lovingly sprinkled with many allegedly 'miraculous' healings.

***

Bert raised his children in the Christian Science faith until they turned 18. He then set them free to choose. Kimberly shopped, but in the end each of them stayed with Christian Science principles and the seeds Bert sewed grew and thrived. Bert's good health philosophy served them well. All three of them remained healthy almost all their lives.

Chapter 4

A Third Choice

With the exception of a minor health scare at the age of 60, Bert was healthy until the age of 75 when a heart attack nearly struck him down for good. But true to form for Bert, he survived and resumed all normal activities -- until it happened again a couple of years later, and again a year after that.

That third attack caused him to have a defibrillator implanted. He loved his life and wasn't yet ready to die.

The defibrillator served him well until Wednesday, March 18, exactly six months into his 80th

year when he had another heart attack. The defibrillator kept his heart going until they could get him to the hospital, but some serious damage was done.

He was left with only two choices: he could have open-heart surgery at the age of 80 which carried a probable survival rate of 60%, or he would need continuous care and monitoring the rest of his life, which meant spending the remainder of his life in a sick bed. To this fun, party-going, golf-playing, bowling, gambling, active guy the very idea of a life in bed was hideous.

His body, which he had always been able to count on, had finally let him down. His faith could no longer heal him.

His heart medications had destroyed his kidneys. He was on dialysis daily. His heart could not support walking. He had been diagnosed with prostate cancer. Other medications made him incontinent.

Bert could not bear the thought of being a burden to everyone around him for the rest of his life. He could not stand the thought of not going to work or not being able to drink.

Open heart surgery or bedridden for life. Not enough choices. Sure enough, leave it to Bert to come up with a third option. Bert chose to 'terminate.'

Chapter 5
Saturday, March 21, late evening

A Realization

"Hi Mom. How are you doing?"
"I'm okay."
"How's Dad today?"
"About the same."
"He's not getting better?"
"No."
"But he's pulled through this before."
"This time is different."
Pause. "How? Different how?"

"It's just different."
"Oh, Mom no! Is Michael there?"
"Yes."
"May I talk to him please?"
There was a pause.
"Hi Kimberly," Michael said.
"Hey, Michael. How's Dad?"
"He's holding steady. Are you coming?"
"I…I don't know."
"This is different than the other times."
"I know... I don't know... I have to think."
"Okay."
"Can I talk to him?"
"He can't really talk. He was intubated and his throat is sore and hoarse."
Sigh. "Okay. How is his spirit?"
"He seems to be shutting down or giving in or something. It's hard to explain."
"Oh no. Is he going to have the surgery?"
"We don't know yet. We may know more by morning."
"Okay."
"We'll talk to you tomorrow, okay?"
"You don't think he'll die tonight, do you?"
"No. I don't think it will be tonight."
"Okay."

Being unmarried and living alone with four cats and a big dog, it's not that easy to jump on a plane and go somewhere, particularly on such short notice and particularly on a Sunday.

I got in bed and turned out the light. As I looked out the window, it seemed an oddly quiet and unusually dark night.

I pulled up the covers and tried to relax but my mind was racing and spinning and there seemed to be something lodged in the pit of my stomach. It felt like a scratchy peach pit. Obviously it was not an actual lump but an emotional reaction. My Dad was the most important, most influential person in my life. The thought that I might lose him was unbearable. I lay in bed and prayed for guidance on what to do.

Then an odd thing happened.

At the time I had a cat named Rudy, a green-eyed, long-haired silver mutt of a smart cat. In the dark, he hopped onto the bed and began to purr loudly, louder than usual it seemed. What he did next surprised me.

With his front paws he felt around my tummy until he located with precision that 'lump' in my gut. With his two front paws, he began to knead right on that spot and didn't stop until the discomfort was gone and I was asleep.

Rudy had never kneaded on me before that night, and he never did after that night.

It is said that cats absorb and dissipate negative energy from their humans. For me on that night, this was true.

Chapter 6

The Beginning

I woke up Sunday morning wondering why I had even hesitated. Of *course* I would go to be with my sick father, whatever it took.

Even on a Sunday, I somehow managed to get the dog boarded, obtain a bereavement fare on the next flight to Chicago and enlist the help of the neighbor who lived in the unit behind me to drive me to the airport. It was a God Thing.

I arrived at Chicago's Midway airport around noon. My luggage even made it there with me. Another God Thing.

Michael met me at the airport in Dad's big Buick. It had been a couple of years since we had seen each other. We shared an emotional hug that lasted a little longer than usual.

I settled in for the 30-minute ride.

"So how is Dad today?" I asked.

"Things have changed since last night," he said.

"Tell me."

He reached over and took my hand. "Dad has decided against the surgery. He is refusing all further medications, and he is having his defibrillator removed."

I felt queasy.

Michael continued through my tears and his. "They moved him to hospice this morning. I'm sorry."

The rest of the thirty-minute ride to the hospital was quiet, but, except for our mutual dismay, it was a comfortable silence.

Michael was the eldest of my two older brothers. He and I had always been comfortable and close, and we were alike in our closeness with Dad. We both knew that once Dad decided something, he rarely changed his mind. We also knew that these were life-ending decisions.

On that ride we shared an unspoken sense of dread, knowing we were about to lose our pillar, our rock, the single most important and influential person in each of our lives.

***

I had not visited Dad for a couple of years. I couldn't wait to see him. He was in a private room on the 5th floor.

When you enter the room a tiny bathroom is immediately to your left, and the bed is across the room with the head of bed to your left. There was a sizeable window on the far wall which offered plenty of light so the room didn't seem like a coffin.

Chairs had been placed at each side of the bed and at the foot of the bed, against the right wall, under a ceiling-mounted TV. What aired on that TV later that night would have a permanent place in my memory.

There was my sweet Dad with his familiar bald head that glistened in the light. By now the ring of hair that ran from one temple around the back of his head to the other temple he called his 'toilet seat' had long since turned grey. We used to ask him why he was bald so young. He explained the Army beds were too short and rubbed all the hair off his head. Whether we believed that or not was up to us.

As a teen, when I wanted to borrow the car, I would stroke his head over and over slowly, slowly. He would drop his eyelids over his hazel eyes and pretend to be hypnotized, and like a sleepwalker hand over the keys. The next day he would ask me how I got the car keys.

"Dad!" I rushed across the room to hug him and kiss his sweet little apple cheek.

"Hi Honey," his smile lit up his eyes like it always did when he saw me. It was one of the many ways I knew he loved me and that I was special to him. I was his only daughter, a Daddy's Girl.

Mom did not get up from her chair by the window. I suspect she did not want to let go of her dying husband's hand. I went around the end of the bed and gave her a hug and kiss.

"How are you doing, Dad? I asked as I took a seat at the end of the bed."

"I'm fine."

His voice was high and hoarse. Seniors sometimes develop this voice from deteriorating vocal cords, but his was from the intubation.

He didn't look too bad. A little thin and a tad pale, but not too bad. He had a wide, stumpy nose, one I am glad I did not inherit. When he blew it he sounded like a tugboat. I think that was just to make us laugh.

He had the oxygen in his nose. There was an IV in the back of his left hand. The monitors that kept track of his heart rate, breathing and blood pressure were stuck all over him, but the monitoring machines were tucked neatly in one corner of the room, barely noticeable and silent. There was also a monitoring station directly across the hall from his room.

Dad was fully coherent. He was able to carry on a conversation and, as always, make us laugh.

Mom enjoyed the conversations. Just the talking. She wanted to fill every silence with talking.

At other times, when he was being tended to or when he was sleeping, she seemed zoned out. She wasn't crying, she just didn't seem to know what to do with herself. I think she had not yet fully realized what was about to happen.

Mom by the window, Michael on Dad's right and me at the foot of the bed, we sat together for an hour or so, the four of us. Dad wanted to know all about us and what was going on in our lives. With only days to live, he was more interested in us than his own state of affairs.

Dad's lunch came. Hospital food, unidentifiable, but he ate it. Mom thought she should try to hand feed him, but he was fine on his own. He wanted more applesauce. He wanted the whole jar. The nurse generously obliged with one additional two-ounce cup but not the entire jar.

As always, Dad kept us laughing. Through Sunday afternoon we were a family minus one; Dirk had not yet decided to make the trip with his family to Chicago from Lexington.

I knew that Dad believed in reincarnation. He believed life on Earth is a school where one comes to learn the lessons God has for you. You reincarnate again and again, each time learning more. (He did not believe you come back as an animal or insect.) Eventually one becomes perfect, in God's image, and incarnate lives are no longer necessary.

When I was a girl Dad and I were strolling a beach. I don't remember where. As we walked along we spotted an empty crab shell.

"See that?" he said. "That's what happens to your body when you die." He toed it over in the sand. "Your body is just an empty shell because the real you, your spirit, is in heaven. Ashes to ashes, dust to dust."

Now we were in a hospice room and that was about to be his truth.

Dad was still his joking self. The mood was light and fun. I asked him a silly question.

"Dad, if you come back as something other than human, what do you want to come back as? I thought he would just smile and chuckle, but he surprised me. He answered suddenly, with certainty.

"A fish!" He blurted the word out in that hoarse voice.

All three of us burst out laughing.

"What? A *fish*? Why in the world would you want to come back as a *fish?*"

He did not answer. His eyes were closed. He was not smiling.

I could not know then the personal significance this comment would later take on.

***

Dirk called.

"Oh hi Dirk," Michael said.

"How is Dad doing?" Dirk asked.

"Since we talked yesterday things have changed. He's decided not to have the surgery. He is also stopping any further medications. He was moved to hospice this morning. He has decided to go, Dirk. I'm sorry."

"Well take him outside! Put him in his wheelchair and roll him around outside! Get him some fresh air! He'll be fine." It was as though Dirk had not even heard what Michael had just told him.

Dirk sounded angry and impatient, but it could have been panic. Dirk and Dad had some rough times while Dirk was growing up. As often happens with two people who struggle with their relationship, when things finally get worked out, the problems they had have a way of making them even closer than they otherwise might be.

"He's getting weaker, Dirk. Are you coming?"

"No, we're going to wait and see how he does." Dirk was in firm denial but I don't think he realized it

"Jason wants to talk to him."

Michael handed the phone to Dad and he and Jason had a short conversation. Lynn spoke with him, too.

***

Through the day Dad would drift off to sleep. Michael and I could tell when he was praying and when he was sleeping. Mom held his hand from her chair by the window, desperately I thought. Among the three of us we made sure someone was there with him holding his hand at all times. He was precious to each of us.

Dad awoke just before dinner. Tenderly, Mom gave him water through the straw.

Just a few moments later an odd thing happened. Dad's eyes began to float. They were open, but unfocused. They seemed to swim. He was not there. I don't know how else to describe it. He was not seizing, not sleeping, not praying, just…not there.

Michael and I looked at each other as if to say, 'Did you see that?' We both knew he was somewhere else in his consciousness and not present with us. Michael pointed to the ceiling. He mouthed, "He's talking to the angels." I nodded in agreement.

It lasted a few minutes. He was silent, his breathing quiet. Soon he stirred, his eyes came back into focus, and he was back with us again. His monitors stayed silent. That was the first time it happened, but it would happen more frequently as the hours passed.

***

Technically Dad was still employed. He had not quit, neither had he retired. He used to say, "You retire, you die."

Dad was on the phone with his office when I returned to the room after a break. Apparently there was some disagreement over who would replace him. Dad wanted his replacement to be a lady who had been at his side for 30 years. The firm wanted it to be a young new starting broker. Despite knowing he would soon no longer be with us, he was still concerned about the quality of service his customers would receive after he was gone.

Dad argued with the person on the other end of the line over this. I have to say it was a rather heated argument, at least on his side of the conversation.

He was quiet for a minute as he listened to the person on the other end.

Suddenly he shouted, "You can't fire me, I *quit*!"

We've had some good laughs in the family over this. He is on his death bed at the age of 80 and he says that.

Since Dad seemed stable for the time being, Michael and I went back to the house. Our absence gave Mom and Dad some privacy. It seems to me there are no two people in the world closer to each other, who know each other better, than a husband and wife. The depth and intimacy of their knowledge of one another is surpassed by no other relationship.

While we were gone Mom and Dad spoke of their memories. Their time together had been 56 years, so they had plenty to talk about.

Because of his sore throat, Dad vocalized as little as possible. He motioned for Mom to raise the automatic bed.

"Want your bed up?" Mom had to reach across Dad to change the setting. She pressed the button and the bed rose up. Immediately he motioned for her to lower it.

"Down again? Okay." Again she reached across him and pressed the button. The bed went down.

With a twinkle in his eye he motioned for her to raise it again. She did.

With a twinkle and a smirk, he promptly motioned for her to lower it.

Suddenly she stopped short. "Wait a minute," she said. Suspicious, she looked him in the eye. Over mischief eyes he raised his bushy little eyebrows twice.

"Oh you! We're having sex now, are we." She poked him and giggled like a schoolkid. So did he.

Dad: still the jokester, no matter how bad he felt. Amazing.

Soon Michael and I returned. Michael held Dad's right hand while Mom held the other. We conversed about various things. Periodically nurses came in to check on him and slip away again. There was an aura of respect among the staff. People spoke quietly and moved silently.

Through the window, the sky was clear and the light was beginning to fade. Mom and Michael had gone down to get something to eat from the cafeteria. I was sitting on the window side finally getting my turn to hold Dad's hand. These were the hands that changed my diapers, taught me to walk and ride a bike, taught me how to use tools, and let me go when it was time.

I asked Dad if he wanted me to read to him from the Bible. I didn't really want to, I just wanted to sit with him. Still, I thought I'd ask.

"Do you want me to read to you Dad?" I picked up his Bible from the bedside table.

He looked in my eyes. His eyes were different somehow. They held a peculiar 'knowing' as if he could read my thoughts.

"No, that's okay," he said.

Somehow he knew I didn't really want to read to him just then. I don't know how he knew, he just knew. It was odd.

The nurses came in to give Dad dialysis. He was quiet for the most part, but a few minutes into it he groaned. It was an audible, pain-filled sound he tried to muffle but could not. I had never heard Dad in pain before. It made me hurt for him. My eyes watered as I pressed the back of his hand to my lips. "I love you Dad," I whispered. He nodded; he knew. I had not realized dialysis was painful. I prayed a silent prayer for him.

Mom and Michael returned after the dialysis was through. Not intentionally, that's just how it happened. Mom turned on the TV. It was the academy awards. Mom chattered away but wasn't getting much response from anyone. I think she was trying to 'be strong' as they say.

Flowing up and down the hallway outside the room was a steady stream of people coming and going, visiting the dying, slowly saying their goodbyes to loved ones. Nuns drifted, occasionally entering a room to comfort family members or pray for the terminally ill.

Out in Hollywood, the Academy was celebrating itself. It all seemed so wrong. My father was dying, yet life was going on as usual. It's strange how some moments etch themselves into one's memory. I will never forget that scene. And each spring of my future, when the Academy Awards show came around, I would forever be reminded of my father's passing.

I kept wondering how this passing was going to happen. Would he have a seizure or another heart attack and suddenly fall over dead? Would he gasp and shake in terror? Would he suddenly stop breathing and fight for air? Would he linger for days, weeks, even months?

I knew only one thing for certain: there was no hope for recovery of any kind. Dad was leaving us.

At that moment I could not bear the grief. I went down the elevator and outside for some air. There I could weep openly.

The day passed with Dad alternately sleeping and joking.

***

Apparently the hospital staff employed only one loud nurse who, promptly at 9 p.m., burst into the room.

"Time for your medication, Mr. Binghamton." She announced it like a Staff Sergeant.

"I don't need that. I'm dying," he said. He pushed the words out hoarsely.

"Not on my watch you're not," she shot back good-naturedly. "Open your mouth."

I suppose Dad thought, 'what difference could it make now.' He took the medication. Dad knew how to get along with the female gender. When asked how he managed such a long marriage, he would answer, "Just say 'Yes dear.'"

Those medications would be the last he would take.

***

It was 10 p.m. and time to leave. There had not been too many things in my life, and I'm sure Michael's too, more difficult than leaving that night. He would be alone all night. All of us wondered silently what anyone would wonder at a moment like that: Would he live through the night. Would we get the call in the night, or would the night pass uneventfully.

Michael leaned over and kissed Dad on the cheek. He took his hand. Talk to your angel tonight, okay Dad?"

Dad nodded 'yes.' I think it took too much effort to talk.

We tearfully said our goodbyes and went back to the house. Michael slept by the phone.

Chapter 7

She Will Lift Me Up

Monday dawned a pretty spring morning, clear and sunny. This helped to ease the fog of sadness that clung to the air around us. Perhaps it was God's way of reassuring us. "I know your pain. I've got him."
    There had been no phone call in the night. Still, there could have been an oversight. We phoned the hospital and to the relief of us all, Dad was awake, had eaten breakfast, and was stable. This news relieved the anxiety and the urgency of getting to the hospital quickly. We had breakfast together around the small table in

Mom's kitchen. I fed bread to Dad's little pet chipmunk that lived under their patio. I felt sad for his future. Dad had been feeding him every morning for years. I feared that Mom, not a renowned animal lover, would not continue the ritual.

We arrived at the hospital around 10. Dirk and his family had phoned earlier in the morning and all three had spoken with Dad. They said he was coherent and seemed normal. Except for his hoarse voice, it seemed to them Dad was not even sick.

After we had greeted Dad and sat with him a little while, two nurses came in. As they were checking on things, Dad said matter-of-factly, "I pooped myself." His medications from the night before had continued his incontinence. Until then, I had not been aware that he was wearing a diaper.

We cleared the room while the nurses cleaned him up. I was sickened by how demeaning and degrading it must be for him. My proud, strong father, reduced to this. No wonder he prayed to die.

When we got the all clear to go back in and Dad was all settled in his bed again, Michael asked Dad a question.

"Did you talk to your angel last night, Dad?"
"Yes," he said.
"Oh really? What did she say?"

Michael was standing over him adjusting his pillows. Dad looked up at him with hope in his eyes like a child looks to a helping parent.

"She said she would lift me up."

There was a surprised pause in the room. Michael spoke next.

"Who?" asked Michael. "Who said that?"

Dad didn't answer.

"Did Lynn say that?"

I think we were all a little surprised that he had actually conversed in words with an angel. Even with our strong faith, at that moment it seemed difficult to believe for some odd reason. Dirk, Lynn and Jason had spoken with Dad earlier, we knew, so Michael thought perhaps Lynn had said something like that.

"Who said she would lift you up, Dad?"

Again, no answer.

***

The day passed slowly. Outside, the birds still chirped, the wind still blew and the sun traveled on.

Dad was in and out, with us and not with us, with increasing frequency. One of his episodes lasted almost ten minutes. In between episodes or 'floats,' he slept, prayed, and yes, even held completely lucid conversations with us, being himself and joking around as much as he could without talking.

His eyes were half open. They began to swim. Michael and I saw what was happening. We remained respectfully quiet. His lips moved briefly, he appeared to stop to 'listen.' He nodded his head. "Okay," he said aloud. His lips moved again, stopped. His words were inaudible to us. His eyes floated.

Suddenly something slashed through the silence like a jagged dagger.

"Oh Honey!" Mom chirped loudly, "remember that time we went to Langford's cabin?"

It was bone-jarring. Dad was instantly yanked back into his body. He looked distressed and frustrated. So was I. I wanted to scold Mom but held my tongue. Michael was ever the patient one.

"Mom," watch when he's communicating with heaven and don't talk then." Gentle but firm.

I understood Mom was anguished. She had only the past to relive, since there was no future with her beloved spouse. The situation had to be so very difficult for her.

Sometime mid-afternoon two tall, important-looking men entered the room. Doctors. They worked over Dad for a few minutes. I leaned into Michael.

"What are they doing?" I whispered.

"Removing his defibrillator."

My heart sighed.

The doctors quietly disappeared. Had he been healthier, Dad would have complained about how much he paid for that thing and what a rip-off it was that now they would re-sell it to someone else.

Later that afternoon Dirk called again. He spoke with Michael and with Dad. Dad never asked Dirk to come. Yet again, Dirk chose not to come. He would call again later that evening.

Dinner came. Dad ate some of it. They had brought him two little cups of applesauce instead of one. He eagerly scarfed them down.

About an hour later I was sitting on Dad's right, holding his hand. He looked over at me and pointed to the ceiling.

"What, Dad?" I asked. "What is it?"

"Bugs!" he said.

"Bugs?" There are bugs on the ceiling?"

"Ants!" he said.

I had heard that seeing bugs that aren't there is common with heart disease. I did not consider this a particularly spiritual experience.

As dusk settled in and the light from the window turned grey, I was still sitting in the same place. I was not holding Dad's hand at the moment.

That's when he began to fly.

Suddenly he looked over at me with glee in his eyes, his face lit up like a child at Disney world for the first time.

"What, Dad?" I asked, "What is it?"

He hooked his thumbs together and flapped his fingers like wings, sailing his hands up and down in the air.

"Flying? You're flying?"

He nodded excitedly.

He closed his eyes. There was a big smile on his face. He seemed to be enjoying the flight. I thought the angels must be taking him on a test ride.

At that moment a small bit of my sadness was replaced with joy. I felt happy for him, certain that he would soon be on his way to heaven, flying high.

How drastically things would turn for the worse in the hours to come!

A few hours had passed when Dirk called again. Still, he had chosen not to come and be with his Dad in his last hours on Earth. It is possible he could not bear to watch his best buddy, his playmate, pass away.

At exactly 7 p.m. the hospital Chaplain came in. He prayed with us. From the Bible we read to Dad his favorite Psalms, 91 and 86.

***

Visiting hours were almost over. I sat at the foot of the bed under the TV, Mom was by the window, and Michael was pulled up in a chair on his right when Dad floated out again. We all held still and quiet, letting the moment happen. I wondered if during one of these trips out of his body he would simply never come back.

In a few minutes Dad nodded his head.

"Yes," he said.

He was quiet. He nodded again.

"Yes, I will," he said solemnly.

His eyes came back into focus. He looked around at us as though surprised we were still there, surprised at where he found himself: in a hospital bed with most of his family around him.

"What happened, Dad? What did you see?"

No answer.

"Dad?"

Still no answer.

He seemed restless. He was not smiling. He was not giggling. For the first time ever, he was not joking with someone.

Mom gently put moistening drops in his eyes. He asked for water. She put the straw to his lips. Sometime during the day he had regained control over his bladder so he was able to use a jar to urinate into.

He asked for the pee jar. We called the nurse and she slipped it under his bedcovers. He did the rest. The nurse took it and returned with a clean jar which she left on the table for us.

We did not like leaving Dad like this. Again, we did not know if we would ever see him alive again. Leaving on this night was even more difficult than leaving the night before. In fact, it was gut-wrenching, particularly given the fact that the hospital chaplain had paid Dad a visit.

We bid so long, lots of kisses and long hugs, see you in the morning. Michael leaned close and kissed his cheek. "Talk to God tonight, Dad. See what He says."

Dad nodded. His eyes were closed. This time he did not smile goodnight. I cannot imagine what was going on inside his head and his heart that night as he watched us go.

It was a quiet ride home, each of us buried inside our own personal grief. For me, that night's sleep was replaced by prayer.

Chapter 8

Go To Hell

Tuesday morning came. Michael phoned the hospital and I think we were all a bit surprised, pleasantly of course, that Dad was still with us.

Michael drove, Mom sat in the front, I sat in back. On the ride to the hospital I wondered what Dad had gone through during the night. So close to death and all alone in the night. I wished the hospital did not limit visiting hours for hospice patients.

When we got to Dad's room the nurses reported that the night had been uneventful. He had not eaten much breakfast. He was weak and slept a lot, but his sleep had been restless in the night.

Outside Dad's window the sun was shining clearly again. Same message from God. It was the kind of morning Dad would have loved. Would it be his last? I wish he could have gone outside.

We had been there about ten minutes when, like the previous morning, Michael asked Dad a question. He put his hands on Dad's chest and asked, "Did you talk to God last night, Dad?"

Dad nodded.

"What did He say?"

"Go to hell!" Dad blurted out the words so strongly that we thought he was kidding and laughed. Later we would find he was not kidding. Not at all.

About an hour passed. It was a still morning.

"I have to poop," Dad said. Evidently in the night he had regained control over his bowels, too. That was quick and was great news.

The nurses got him out of bed and helped him into a potty chair. I had not realized how thin he was until I saw him out from under the covers. I could see the bones and ribs in his back. Normally a robust 5'8" 165 pounds, his illness over the previous few months had withered him to below 110 pounds.

As Mom and I were leaving the room to give him some privacy, Dad had his back to us as he sat on the potty chair. Michael squatted down in front of him and put his hands on Dad's knees. He looked up into Dad's eyes.

"How are you feeling, Dad?" Michael's heart was wide open. You could hear it in his voice and see it in his eyes. "How are you feeling?"

"Befuddled."

I gasped inside. It felt like something pinched my heart. That moment had the sharpest edge of all, for two reasons.

It was his use of the word 'befuddled' and not 'bewildered' or 'baffled' or 'confused. Throughout my fifty years with Dad, it was characteristic of him to pop out with a completely unexpected word at a completely unexpected time. For example, referring to the mischief we caused as teenagers as 'debauchery.' This gave us hysterical giggles. Not only did we not know yet what it meant, but it seemed like such a big, sophisticated word at a time when we were about to be grounded for a year.

Secondly, having watched over him for the past two days, I knew that part of him -- in his head -- he was in another world, another dimension, seeing other people and conversing back and forth with others we could not see or hear, yet his body and who he had always been remained on Earth in that hospital room with us. It was eerie.

And I knew what he meant. I knew exactly what he meant by 'befuddled.' Dad had an extremely close relationship with God. He thought of God as his friend. In life, Bert was well-liked and had many friends – real and true friends. He could ask anything of any one of them and they would be there to grant him the favor. They knew also that the favor would be returned. He just had that kind of integrity in him and people knew it.

Now, Dad thought he could simply ask God to come home now and God would take him home. He didn't realize it would take so long and be so difficult.

They say the process of birth and the process of death are equally as difficult.

***

The morning crept along slowly. He no longer had the oxygen in his nose. We savored every last moment with him. Dad was out more than he was in now.

That's when he began to climb the stairway.

His eyes were closed. With his right arm, he reached up and forward at a 45 degree angle. Then he slowly brought his arm back down to his side. He reached up again. Again, he brought his arm back. His hand was open and flat, as if pulling himself up by a handrail too wide to grasp.

Rhythmically, even dutifully, he climbed. Up and back, up and back. It looked as though he was climbing stairs that were too big to climb easily.

Nurses whispered in and out of the room. His eyes remained closed. He was unaware of them or us. We did not disturb him. He continued to 'climb' for close to an hour.

At last he stopped climbing. He came back into his body, but only briefly. He looked around, at the room, at us…and floated out again.

He nodded his head. "Yes," he said aloud, "okay." Then he got quiet, as if listening.

Suddenly, he spoke in a surprisingly normal voice.

"How do you get on?" he said. We knew he was not talking to us.

I looked questioningly at Michael.

He leaned in to me and whispered. "There is a theory or belief that there are carts that drive around heaven and pick people up and take them to the Throne of God."

I had not heard that. I do not know where that theory comes from or what religion holds it. It seemed to make sense. He was asking how to get on the carts.

He 'listened'. He nodded. He 'listened.'

Suddenly he shot his hand into the air, like a kid in a classroom who knows he has the correct answer. "Cancer! I have cancer!" he shouted.

He stopped and listened. He nodded. "Okay," he said aloud.

It was as if Dad was in a crowd of people and someone was questioning the crowd, asking what reason they were there, standing at the gate. Dad had prostate cancer.

It was after he eagerly volunteered that he had cancer that he grew quiet for a very long time. Perhaps an hour passed. We thought he was sleeping, but apparently not.

Suddenly he blurted out in a surprisingly loud, almost impatient voice, "What's the matter with Dirk?! He thinks if you game it you win the Pepsi prize!"

We think Dad was waiting for Dirk. He loved us all so much and wanted to say goodbye to each of us.

Each of us knows what we can handle and what we cannot handle emotionally. If Dirk chose not to be there for Dad, whether consciously or subconsciously, for

his decision I neither blame him nor judge him. Everyone is different and must act
    according to his heart.

While Dad was quiet, I took some time to visit the chapel. I sat and prayed for Dad's deliverance, for Mom's grief, for Dad's comfort in his struggle.

When I emerged from the chapel door, there was a family gathered all together on the bench on the opposite side of the narrow hallway. In their arms they held a newborn baby. I sat down across from them to watch. They were so happy. I was happy for them but so unhappy for us. The baby's family and my family stood at opposite ends of the spectrum of emotion and of life.

A new baby. Life. The old making way for the new. Life just circles around and around. One lost, one born.

When I returned to the room Dad was quiet. He was not sleeping, he was out of his body, just out of reach, floating between his bed and the other side above.

After about twenty minutes he returned to us. Just as he did, the phone rang.

It was Dirk. His son Jason wanted to call Dad at nine that evening so they could talk. Bert was his only grandfather and his favorite person. Jason love him to pieces. The call was arranged and agreed on.

Two hours passed before the unthinkable came to pass.

Chapter 9

Last Call

It began with an animalistic moan. Then another, louder moan. He called out, "NO!" He groaned again, more urgently this time.

"Oh no, noooo!" Increased urgency in his voice. "I can't!"

"What, Dad? What is it?"

No answer.

With his hands he began to pull at his hospital gown. He was trying to tear his clothes off, trying to get undressed. He was panicked.

"I'm burning! I'm on fire!"

"No, Dad, you're not on fire. You're fine."

Dad tried to leap from the bed and flee in panic and fear. It was all Michael could do to keep him in the bed.

"I'm on fire! My clothes are on fire! I'm burning!" He almost screamed. He was throwing himself around and struggling and flailing his arms. He almost hit Michael in the face.

Michael kept at him, calming him -- or trying.

"Dad, here's your gown, see?" He held the gown between his fingers. "See? You're not on fire. It's not burning."

"I'm going to explode! I can't! I can't explode *here*! Nooo! I can't!"

"Dad, Dad. You're not going to explode. You are in a hospital room. You are not on fire," I said.

"It's so hot. I'm burning!"

Michael struggled to keep Dad from completely undressing.

"Dad, we're here with you. You're not on fire. You are here with us."

"The bed! The bed's on fire! Get away! Got to get away!"

"Dad. Dad. The bed is not on fire."

"It's burning!"

I had never seen my father fearful of anything. Now here was my happy-go-lucky, fun-loving, giddy Daddy throwing himself around his death bed in a raw, gut-ripping frenzy of dread and panic and horror. What was he seeing? Where was he? He was living through unimaginable horror and there was absolutely nothing we could do, nothing. We had to let it happen.

I stood up and put my hands on his legs. Mom put her hands on his body. We all put our hands on him hoping our touch would bring him out of his terrifying ordeal and back to this hospital bed and this moment.

Dad was hyperventilating raw, ragged breaths. Struggling, panicked. This time his monitors must have gone off. I'm sure his respiration, heart rate and blood pressure had spiked through the roof. A nurse started to enter the room. She wore a look of concern. She must have heard all the shouting. Michael looked back at her. "We're fine. Thank you." The nurse respectfully, quickly, left again and quietly closed the door behind her. This was a very private moment, indeed.

"Dad. Dad."

"NO!! I can't! I'm going to explode! I can't! I can't!"

"We are right here, Dad. You are not going to explode. We're right here," Michael repeated, but it made no difference. Dad continued to struggle.

He stopped shouting, but continued to moan and struggle for close to thirty minutes. Thirty minutes is an eternity to watch a dearly loved one engulfed in such intense dread. Like the sharp edge of a knife cutting away at your heart.

Gradually, little by little, we began to succeed in calming him down. The moaning faded to a strange whimpering sound. He finally stopped trying to tear off his clothing. He stopped thinking he was going to explode. He stopped thinking he was on fire. His breathing began to normalize, but he was still panting.

"Dad. Dad?"

"Um-hm." Finally, the first lucid response in an endless thirty minutes.

As we had mistakenly thought, Dad had not been joking when he said God told him to go to hell. It appeared he had done just that. He had seen hell.

We gave him water. We straightened his blankets and pillows. He settled down. We prayed with him. Mom continued her zombie expression, as if she wasn't even there. It was possible the horror of the previous half hour triggered an emotional shutdown for her own self-preservation.

At long last Dad settled into resting state. For two and a half days he had been on his back. Now, for the first time, he was on his side, facing out the window. He appeared to be out of body and not sleeping or praying. We waited. We prayed among ourselves. When we weren't praying, each of us was experiencing our own private horror at the thought that our loving Papa was being sent to hell.

About an hour passed. He stayed in that state, that place between heaven and Earth, for the full hour. By now it was early evening and the light outside the window was fading. The world carried on, oblivious of the scene playing out in Dad's small hospital room.

Then, strangely, we noticed Dad's lips moving. He was whispering aloud. His eyes were closed. He was repeating something again and again. We could not decipher what he was saying.

I whispered to Michael. "Can you hear what he's saying?"

He shook his head. He stood up, leaned over and put his ear by Dad's lips. He listened for a few seconds. He turned back smiling broadly.

"'It's so beautiful.' He's saying 'it's so beautiful.'"

Dad, eyes closed, was repeating over and over again, no punctuation, just a stream of words, "It's so beautiful it's so beautiful it's so beautiful it's so beautiful it's so beautiful!" The beatific expression on his old face seemed to smooth away the age. He radiated joy. You could almost physically feel it coming off him.

Only two times in my life had I seen my father cry; once when his mother passed and once when our dog died. Now a single tear emerged from the corner of his eye and slipped quietly down his cheek. I tried to think if, in my own life, I had ever seen a sight so lovely it made me weep. A mountain, a starry sky, an ocean view, the clouds in the sky. I had not.

For a full minute he whispered under his breath, repeating those three words.

Soon his whispers faded and he fell into a deep and restful sleep. There was an identifiable difference between when he was sleeping, praying or floating. Right now he was sleeping. Very deeply, very restfully, very calmly, very peacefully.

He was stable again. It was just after 7 p.m.

Earlier in the day Dad had asked for his hearing aids. Now, for reasons known only to Mom, she insisted we go back to the house right then to find them for him.

We could make it there and back in about 45 minutes. We did not wish to go and leave Dad at this particular time, but Mom insisted.

Chapter 10

I Really Have To Go

At home, Michael quickly called Helen while I looked everywhere I could think of for his hearing aids. In his dresser, in his bedside table, in the junk drawer in the kitchen, in the bathroom medicine cabinet, in the drawer of the table beside his reading chair. Nothing. I was unsuccessful. So was Michael with the few places he also looked. We gave up; we had to get back.

We raced through a Wendy's drive-through for a drink to go. Michael drove a little faster than he should up the long County Line Road that led to the hospital. The sun had set and it was dark. We were almost at the stop sign where you turn left. Suddenly and without warning, in the very center of my solar plexus, a flash bomb exploded. I looked at the clock. It was 8:30.

"Hurry, Michael," I said urgently.

Left turn. ¼ block. Right turn. Up and over the bridge that arched over the railroad tracks. Left into the hospital parking lot. Up the elevator for what seemed a very long ride. We leaped off the elevator, went 20 feet left, turned right – and two nurses stopped us there. Oh no.

"He's gone?"

The nurse nodded. "I'm so sorry."

I suddenly felt all scrambled inside and not in a good way. You think you are prepared. You're not. You think you have steeled yourself for that last, very final strike to your heart. You have not. I don't think there is a way to prepare.

Just over an hour after seeing indescribable beauty, Ischemic Dilated Cardiomyopathy caused his death. Heart disease. Time of death: 8:30.

The hourglass was drained of sand. Bert Binghamton had completed is life.

***

Hospital personnel directed us into a small, dimly-lit gathering room, measuring perhaps twelve by fifteen feet. There were benches along the right wall and a row of chairs along the other wall. At the front of the room was an altar and a kneeling bar.

On the bench on the right side of the room sat Mom. She was crying. She looked so small and withered, sitting there all alone. Her face was distorted and puffy.

Michael sat down next to her and put his arm around her shoulders. I kneeled in front of her. I took her hands in mine.

Suddenly she ripped her hands from mine and jerked away from me as if I were Satan himself. She shrieked a sound I had never heard come out of any human being and never would again.

"Your hands are so cold like his are gonna be!" she screamed at the top of her lungs.

It was so loud and unexpected it sort of blew me back from her. The people in the outer room looked in our direction. I had been holding my soft drink in my hands and yes, my hands were cold.

She was out of her mind with shock and panic and grief. I cannot imagine what she went through in the few minutes that passed between the time Dad died and the time we got there. Here was a woman who, as a young woman, went straight from her father's arm to her husband's arm. She was never on her own. She had never learned how to be alone and independent of another.

She rejected me, but fell into Michael's arms. She was weeping uncontrollably. I could only sit across the room and stay out of it, out of her space, out of her shock, invisible. Michael tried his best to comfort her, but she was inconsolable.

Twenty minutes passed. The nurses came to let us know Dad was ready for viewing.

The bedclothes had been neatly straightened and smoothed over his little body. All monitors had been removed from him and all machines has been removed from the room. The lights had been dimmed. Mom went around the bed and took up her station by the window, now dark.

There was my beloved father, lying dead beneath a dim spotlight.

I kissed his little cheek for the last time. It was still warm. Michael bent to kiss Dad and gave Mom a hug as she sat in her chair. He came around the end of the bed to me and we clung to each other for a long time, drawing comfort and weeping for our lost hero.

We had missed his passing by three minutes. We didn't know if he couldn't wait, or if he planned it that way – it began with just the two of them, and would end with just the two of them.

Later we asked Mom what had transpired.

"I was sitting there with him. Everything was quiet. He said, 'I love you,' and went back to sleep.

I thought he was still sleeping when he spoke in a quiet voice. 'Honey, I've really got to go,' he said. I said, 'Well the jar is around here somewhere,' thinking he meant he had to pee. But something made me look at his face. His eyes were almost double their normal size and just – well – translucent sort of. They just glowed with an inner light. It was eerie. It's hard to describe. A couple of seconds after he said that the nurses rushed into the room. "He's gone," they said. They made me leave the room with them."

He did not have to pee. He had to cross the veil.

Dad's fervent prayers had been answered. God had finally called him home. At long last our Heavenly Father, in His mercy and grace, opened the gate for His precious child.

Chapter 11

The After-ness

In Dad's hospital room Mom, Michael and I sat gathered around his body. I thought of the empty crab shell.

I admit I looked at the ceiling. I did. I had read many accounts of near death experiences of people floating at the ceiling after leaving their bodies. I hoped I could see him, still there, still smiling and laughing, floating above us.

Mom had stopped crying for the moment. Michael was asking her about the arrangements.

Just then the phone rang. Michael picked it up. It was Jason, as had been arranged.

"Jason. How are you?" He paused to listen.

"Jason, I'm so sorry but Grandad passed away."

Again, a pause.

"About 20 or 30 minutes ago."

"Jason? Jason, you there?"

Dirk got on the line.

"Hi Dirk. Yes, we are sitting with him now."

They talked just briefly and the call ended.

The longer we sat with Dad's body the more uncomfortable I became. It was not him. It was an empty vessel, the one God Himself had long ago created to cradle a grateful spirit for 80 years.

I left the hospital to get some fresh air – and to break down. I walked around the parking lot and wept and talked to Dad. By the time I got back, all the doors were locked. Visiting hours were over. The only open door was the emergency room entrance.

It took 35 minutes to convince the people at the desk that I was not there to bomb the hospital, I only wanted to get back to my Dad and my family. But, rules are rules.

***

That night after putting Mom in bed for the first time without Dad beside her, Michael and I lay in our twin beds in Mom's little guest room. The light from the streetlight outside traced faint patterns on the walls.

I tossed and turned and could not sleep. I was thinking of what we had yet to face -- the service, the reception, the people who didn't really feel the depth of your pain or understand at all the physicality of your grief.

The day after that, life would go on as it should, but I did not want it to. Like a child, I wanted him back. How would I ever do without my Dad, my soft place to fall? I wanted things to be the way they had always been.

Michael was quiet and still. I sensed he was probably not asleep.

"I'm keeping you awake, aren't I?"

"No, I'm awake." His voice floated through the dark.

"I don't think I can stand going to the reception tomorrow."

"Okay. Why?" he asked gently.

"I mean, everyone saying 'so sorry for your loss.' I know they are paying their respects, but it all just seems so shallow compared to what we just witnessed. Like going from Rachmaninoff to the Spice Girls."

"I know what you mean."

"You're stronger than I am. I don't think I can go. I just can't face it."

"Okay. I know. It's alright. I'll explain to them you had to get back for work, which you do."

"I was here for the part that counted."

"Yes you were."

Michael understood. I knew Dad would forgive me, and I knew God would forgive me; He knows my heart and how much pain I was in.

There was a pause. An owl hooted softly outside. What Michael said next surprised me.

"Do you think he went to hell?" His voice was heavy with worry and concern.

"No, I don't think that at *all*. He went to heaven. Why would you think he went to hell?

"All that about being on fire and blowing up."

Michael, Dad's entire life message was love. Love of God, love of family. Yes, he was racist and bigoted at times. We are all sinners and make mistakes. But he always taught us God first, the other fellow second, yourself last. His message was love, and God's message is Love."

"But his drinking…"

"I still think that in God's world, Dad's life message of love and faith would override the small mistakes he might have made here on Earth, including his drinking. Maybe those mistakes were the lessons he needed to learn in this life. I just don't think God would toss down someone with such deep devotion and faith and love for God."

"You're right. I guess it's what he said last that counts. '*It's so beautiful.*'"

"Yes! You saw how he was radiating inner light. You saw how his face looked so young. That was the Holy Spirit in him. That came *after* all of the horror. When we left him he was peaceful. 45 minutes later he was gone."

"That's true."

"I think God reassured us by showing us that. And what Mom said about his eyes. His eyes wouldn't glow with a beautiful light if he had gone to hell. If he was being sent to hell, do you think he would have died right then and there when he thought he was on fire, or…?"

Michael sighed with what sounded like relief. "Yes," he said, "you're right. You're right. He didn't just talk God's love, he lived it…with a few slip-ups."

Even in the dark I knew he was grinning. We shared a laugh.

"Yes, just a few slips-ups. But he's in heaven right now, smiling down on us, telling us not to worry."

"Yes he is."

Chapter 12

A Fish and Unexpected Visits

I flew back to Houston late the next day. I wept for the entire three-hour flight. Put my head down on my knees and wept. My seatmate put his hand on my back and asked if I was okay. That was nice. The flight attendants knew this was a bereavement flight and were respectful of me and my uncontrollable tears.

My friend met me at the airport. Again, even my baggage made it back with me. It was dusk. On the car ride home she asked, "So how's your Dad?"

"He passed away."

"OH!" She was shocked. "I thought he was just sick and would get better."

"Not this time."

"I'm so sorry."

"I know. Thank you. It's okay. He wanted to go, so that makes things easier."

By the time my friend dropped me off it was dark.

I lived in a four-plex condo. My unit faced a shallow creek. From the parking lot to my front door, you had to walk the length of the entire building, past my neighbor's front door, around the corner and then south the full width of the building to my own front door.

Precisely as I reached the corner near my door, I stopped in my tracks. A huge fish jumped in the creek. *Ker-SPLOOSH!* I couldn't see the fish, but I could tell by the sound of the splash it was a big one.

"Dad?" I said aloud. "Dad? Is that you?"

The fish jumped again. I could not help but smile and giggle out loud. Now I understood why Dad had said he would come back as a fish.

I lived in that little condo for five years. Never to that point and never again after that did I hear a fish jump in that creek. It was simply too small and shallow for a fish that size. I have never had a hallucination and I was not having one then.

***

Over the next year I had nine visits from Dad in the form of dreams.

While I was away, there had been a terrible and tragic bus crash in the U.S. and many children were killed. That night I dreamed about Dad. I saw him kneeling on the clouds. He was reaching down through the clouds for something that was below him. There was a very large angel standing next to him, overseeing. The angel turned and acknowledged me, making direct eye contact. I asked her, "What is he doing?" She answered, "He is helping the children into heaven."

While he was alive, one of the favorite things between Dad and I was to talk on the phone together. While at work at his desk, or at night at home, he always had time for me and my blabbering.

In one of my dreams we were talking on the phone. At that time there were enormous wildfires burning out of control in Mexico. The prevailing wind was to the north, up across Texas.

In the dream, Dad asked me a question.

"So," he said, "are you getting the smoke from those fires in Mexico?"

Details like this are God's way of reassuring me that my dreams about Dad are literally visits from the other side.

After Dad's departure our family was never again as close as we had been while he was alive. Dad had been the glue that held us together.

A year passed before it dawned on Mom that we had lost our father, so blinded and tunnel-visioned was she under the suffocating weight of her own grief.

The death of her husband was not something Mom could handle. She never really came out from under it. Five years later her eyes would still well up at even a brief mention of his name. On the surface she knew he was in heaven waiting for her, but, sadly, Mom never had a real and true *relationship* with God, so she was unable to receive the gift of His Comfort.

Afterword

There are so many things I don't know, and I have so many questions I don't even know how to ask.

I wonder why it appeared that God sent Dad to hell before He took him to heaven. I asked myself, Was it his cursing? His bigotry? His judgments of others? His racism?

I wonder why Dad refused to tell us who he was talking to and what he was witnessing and seeing. I later wondered this aloud to a friend. She is an extremely devout person who can quote an accurate Scripture verse for just about any situation, and seems to know the Bible inside and out. She said, "God doesn't want us to know. He wants us to rely on faith."

I wonder how it was that, during those last three days, it seemed Dad had acquired a spiritual Knowing. He seemed to know everything – not only what we were thinking, but what Dirk was thinking a thousand miles away.

What I do not question or doubt is that we had been blessed with a glimpse of the other side. It was proof that there is life after death.

I witnessed the courageous, brave and mighty struggle of a big-hearted, God-loving sinner to be with his Creator. Here was a man who repented his sins every day in his nightly prayer. He was not a man to rush to be saved. He loved his God and his God loved him. A lifetime of answered prayers told him Jesus would be there to greet him, and he would go to God through Jesus, right there at the gates of heaven.

In the world of Bert Binghamton, God is a gentle God. God mercifully granted His precious child the early entry for which he had, in his last days, so fervently prayed. At long last this man who had never been baptized, never been 'saved', and whose time was not yet over was welcomed, through the Lord's Grace, into the gates of Heaven.

I am but waiting for you, for an interval, somewhere very near, just round the corner. All is well.

— Henry Michael Holland, 1847

While you have gone to be with others, your loving ways reflect in us. Thank you, Dad.

www.ingramcontent.com/pod-product-compliance
Lightning Source LLC
Chambersburg PA
CBHW022021290426
44109CB00015B/1265